Beginner

Teacher's Resourc

New Headway
English Course

Mark Uribe
Liz and John Soars

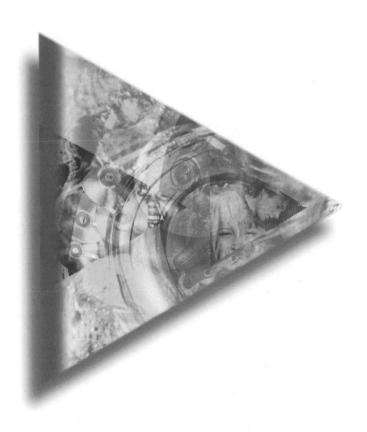

Beginner

OXFORD
UNIVERSITY PRESS

OXFORD
UNIVERSITY PRESS

Great Clarendon Street, Oxford OX2 6DP

Oxford University Press is a department of the University of Oxford.
It furthers the University's objective of excellence in research,
scholarship, and education by publishing worldwide in

Oxford New York

Auckland Bangkok Buenos Aires Cape Town Chennai
Dar es Salaam Delhi Hong Kong Istanbul Karachi Kolkata
Kuala Lumpur Madrid Melbourne Mexico City Mumbai Nairobi
São Paulo Shanghai Singapore Taipei Tokyo Toronto

with an associated company in Berlin

Oxford and Oxford English are registered trade marks of
Oxford University Press in the UK and in certain other countries

© Oxford University Press 2002

The moral rights of the author have been asserted

Database right Oxford University Press (maker)

First published 2002
Second impression 2002

ISBN 0 19 4376354

Printed in Spain by Mateu Cromo, S.A. Pinto (Madrid)

Acknowledgements

Illustrations by:
Adrian Barclay pp9, 11, 25, 29, 50, 51, 69; Kathy Baxendale pp27, 37;
Kate Charlesworth p73; Alison Everitt pp33, 55; Phil Garner/Beehive
pp63, 71; Neil Gower pp43, 44; Joanna Kerr p77; Tim Slade pp7, 41;
Harry Venning pp39, 59, 65

**The publisher would like to thank the following for their kind
permission to reproduce photographs:**
Corbis UK Ltd p17 (smiling boy); Eyewire p17 (smiling woman);
The Image Bank p57 (young Hispanic man/Nicolas Russell); Stone
pp17 (businessman/David Hanover), 57 (smiling woman/Chris
Bale); Telegraph Colour Library p17 (doctor/Adam Smith), 21
(teenagers/V. C. L.)

Introduction

This Teacher's Resource Book contains thirty-three photocopiable activities and further ideas for you to use with *New Headway Beginner*. It is a completely new component for the Headway series and has been written with two aims in mind:

- to give teachers additional material that revises and extends the work in the Student's Book

- to give students lots of extra speaking practice!

Students at beginner level need lots of vocabulary and grammar input. Controlled skills work is also important to develop their reading, writing, listening and speaking. But at the same time, it is also essential that they are given opportunities to 'get active' and actually use their English in meaningful and relevant contexts.

The activities in this book are designed to help your students do this. They encourage students to talk about themselves, compare opinions and views about the world, and practise the kind of situations they are likely to encounter in real life.

In addition, every activity involves an element of team work. Students will need to work together to share or check information, and agree outcomes or solutions. In other words, every activity encourages purposeful interaction where students need to speak and listen to each other.

Through role-plays, language games, questionnaires, and information-gap activities, students are also given the chance to build their confidence and introduce a more personal dimension to their learning.

How to use the photocopiable activities

Each activity starts with the following information:

Aim	the main focus of the activity
Language	the grammar/function exploited
Skills	Speaking, Reading, Writing, and/or Listening
Lesson link	suggestion for when to use the worksheet
Materials	notes for preparation of worksheets

Pre-activity

These activities act as a warm-up before the students carry out the main activity. They act to remind students of the necessary language needed and to set the context. Often they are optional, particularly if following straight on from the lesson in the Student's Book.

Procedure

This section has step-by-step instructions for carrying out the main activity. Each main activity takes between fifteen and thirty minutes and is suitable for most class sizes. (There are additional notes for larger classes.) For each activity there is a photocopiable worksheet. Some of the worksheets need to be cut up before handing out to students.

Extension

After each main activity, there is a suggestion for an extension activity. These are generally writing activities which build on the language or topics covered in the main activity. These can be assigned for homework.

Contents

Worksheet	Description	Language
9.1 **Where were you?**	Interviewing classmates about their whereabouts last Saturday	*was/were*
9.2 **Sorry I'm late!**	Board game to make excuses for being late or early for a party	Past Simple
9.3 **Word search**	Finding words hidden in a word grid	Ordinal numbers; The alphabet; Work and freetime
10.1 **A love story**	Ordering pictures and writing the story	Past Simple irregular verbs
10.2 **Did you have a good holiday?**	Asking and answering about holidays	Past Simple questions; Irregular verbs; *both*
11.1 **Can you . . . ?**	Asking and answering about abilities	*Can you . . . ?* *Yes, I can. / No, I can't.*
11.2 **Yes, of course.**	Making and responding to requests	*Can I/you . . . ?* *Yes, of course.* *I'm sorry. I can't.*
12.1 **Dreams**	Interviewing classmates about their dreams/aspirations	*Would you like to . . . ?* *Yes, I would. / No, I wouldn't.*
12.2 **A delicious dinner!**	Playing a game with picture cards of delicious and horrible dishes	*would like;* Food
12.3 **What would you like?**	Role-playing ordering a meal in a restaurant	*would like;* Food
13.1 **What's happening?**	Marking statements about a picture *true* or *false* from memory	Present Continuous *There is/are . . .*
13.2 **What's the matter?**	Making suggestions	*What's the matter?* *Why don't you . . . ?* *Sorry, I can't help.*
14.1 **Going to Paris**	Ordering pictures and writing the story	Present Continuous for future
14.2 **Sentence search**	Finding sentences hidden in a word grid	Review
14.3 **Whose day is it?**	Matching two halves of a text	Review

1.1

Aim
To find out the name of things in English

Language
What's this in English?
It's a . . .

Skills
Speaking

Lesson link
Use after *What's this in English?* SB p10

Materials
One copy of the worksheet cut up per class of fifteen students. A blank piece of paper per pair of students and dictionaries for the Extension

Pre-activity (5 minutes)

- Pre-teach *table, chair, window, door,* and *pen.* Point to each item in the classroom and ask: *What's this in English?* Elicit/Teach *It's a … .* Drill the question and answer for the items with the class. Make sure students use the contracted form *It's* and the article.

Procedure (15 minutes)

- Give each student a picture card.

- Students mingle showing their cards and asking each other: *What's this in English?* After each exchange, students swap cards and move on to the next student. Go around listening, making sure students are asking and answering the question correctly.

- Encourage students to help each other if they can't remember the name of the item. If neither student can remember, they should come and ask you: *What's this in English?*

Extension (15 minutes)

- Hold up an object the students don't know in English, e.g. your watch. Encourage students to ask you: *What's this in English?* Drill the answer: *It's a watch.*

- Divide students into pairs and give each pair a piece of paper. Ask students, in their pairs, to draw a picture of an everyday object that they would like to know in English. Students then look up the word in their dictionaries and write it on the other side of the piece of paper. Go around helping, checking spelling and pronunciation.

- Students, in their pairs, mingle showing their card (picture side) to another pair and saying: *This is a … .* Then they ask: *What's this in English?* When the other pair of students both correctly answer: *It's a … ,* pairs swap cards and move on to the next pair. Go around listening, making sure students are asking and answering the question correctly.

1 Bingo

3			
	12	20	19
6		28	

2 Bingo

3			19
	30		13
		2	11

3 Bingo

30		18	
6		15	
	1		26

4 Bingo

12		28	
24	16		
4			25

5 Bingo

	30		
24		14	13
	16		8

6 Bingo

20	6		
			14
	8	17	25

7 Bingo

	14	5	
	21		8
23		9	

8 Bingo

1	15		
		5	23
10			7

9 Bingo

2			4
17		11	
	22	25	

10 Bingo

	21		
18	26	9	27
29			

11 Bingo

17			7
		27	
22	10		29

12 Bingo

24	16	14	
	19		
		12	23

3.1

Where's he from?

Aim

To practise asking and answering questions

Language

Present Simple third person questions

Skills

Speaking and Writing

Lesson link

Use after *What's her job?* SB p18 & 19

Materials

One copy of the worksheet cut in half per pair of students. A picture of a famous person (optional). Make a blank ID card per pair of students and provide dictionaries for the Extension

Pre-activity (10 minutes)

- Show the class a picture of a famous person (or write the name of a famous person on the board). Write the following categories on the board: *country, address, phone number, age, job, married.* Elicit questions for each category from the class: *Where's (name) from? What's his/her address? What's his/her phone number? How old is he/she? What's his/her job? Is he/she married?* As each question is asked, encourage students to tell you (or invent) the answer. Write the answers on the board.

- Using the answers on the board, drill the questions again, checking pronunciation and intonation. Say, e.g. *Spain* and encourage students to ask: *Where's he/she from?*, etc.

Procedure (15 minutes)

- Explain that students are going to exchange information to complete ID cards for four people.

- Divide students into pairs. Give Students A worksheet A, and Students B worksheet B. Give students time to look at the worksheet and to check any items of vocabulary.

- In their pairs, students take it in turns to ask and answer questions to complete the missing information in the ID cards. Tell them to use the person's name in their first question to make it clear who they are asking about and then *he, she, his,* or *her* as appropriate in their other questions. Go around listening, helping and correcting as necessary.

- Check the answers with the class. Write the complete ID cards on the board for students to check.

Extension (10 minutes)

- Give each pair of students a blank ID card and ask them to complete the details with any information they choose. Encourage students to use dictionaries to find new jobs and countries.

- Group two pairs together. Pairs take it in turns to hold up their ID card and say: *This is (name).* The other pair ask questions to find out all about the person. Go around listening, helping and correcting as necessary.

A

Hello! _____ _____ is Nikos _____
_____ _____ from Athens. _____
_____ _____ I'm a student. _____
_____ _____ sister and her _____
_____ _____ . She has a _____
_____ . She's a teacher. _____ _____
is in the centre _____ _____ . It's near
_____ _____ . Alex isn't married
_____ _____ _____ a boyfriend.
_____ _____ _____ pop group and
_____ _____ _____ . He has a
_____ _____ _____ .

_____ _____ and I have _____ _____ _____
in town. _____ _____ have a big _____ _____ the country.
_____ _____ two dogs. _____ _____ is a taxi _____
_____ _____ mother is _____ _____ .

✄ ---

B

_____ ! My name _____ _____
and I am _____ _____ . I'm eighteen
and _____ _____ _____ . I have a
_____ _____ _____ name is Alex.
_____ _____ _____ good job.
_____ _____ _____ . Her school
_____ _____ _____ _____
of town. _____ _____ my university.
_____ _____ _____ but she has
_____ _____ . He's in a _____
_____ _____ he's from Germany.
_____ _____ lot of CDs.

My sister _____ _____ _____ a small flat _____ _____ .
Our parents _____ _____ _____ house in _____ _____ .
They have _____ _____ . My father _____ _____ _____
driver and my _____ _____ a doctor.

4.2

Aims
To spell and guess the spelling of words
To write a text using a set of words

Language
Alphabet
Numbers 1–30
Pronunciation

Skills
Speaking, Listening, and Writing

Lesson link
Use after *The alphabet* SB p30

Materials
One copy of the worksheet cut in half per pair of students

Pre-activity (5 minutes)

- Choose two words which students know which can make a two-word crossword, e.g. *student* and *sandwich*. Draw the crossword on the board.

- Invite students to call out letters of the alphabet at random. If the letter is in either of the words, write the letter in the corresponding blank(s). If not, write the letter by the side of the crossword. Continue until both words have been completed or students can guess what the words are from the letters already filled.

Procedure (20 minutes)

- Explain that students are going to play battleships to each find nine words. Draw a small battleships grid on the board and write in two or three words, e.g.

	B	X	I	D	L	S	E
14				D			
23		S	C	H	O	O	L
7			A		G		
18			R				
21			O				
5			L				

- Ask: *What's the letter in D–23?* Encourage students to call out: *H.* Repeat this several times. Then point to a letter in the grid, e.g. *L,* and encourage students to call out the question: *What's the letter in E–23?* Then ask: *What's the letter in B–14?* and elicit/teach: *No letter.*

- Divide students into pairs. Give Student A worksheet A, and student B worksheet B. Tell students not to show each other their worksheets.

- Sitting opposite each other, students take it in turns to ask and answer about locations on the battleships grid. Go around listening, helping and correcting as necessary.

- The first student to get all nine words wins.

Extension (20 minutes)

- Individually, students write a paragraph using the nine words they found in their partner's grid. Go around, helping and correcting as necessary.

- When students have finished, display all the texts written by Students A together, and all the texts by Students B together. Allow students time to read the texts to see how each student used the words.

A

Ask Student B questions and find nine words in this grid, e.g. *What's the letter in H–7 ?*

	E	C	A	H	I	S	G	Y	J	R
13										
7										
11										
19										
14										
22										
28										
30										
5										
16										

Answer Student B's questions about the letters in this grid.

	F	R	N	O	X	K	B	U	Q	Y
15		M								
10	B	R	A	Z	I	L		M		
9		R						A		
21		C	H	I	L	D	R	E	N	
24	T	W	O					I		
16	A		H	U	S	B	A	N	D	
27	X							U		
8	I		D	R	I	V	E	R		
29								S		
3								E		

✂ ---

B

Answer Student A's questions about the letters in this grid.

	E	C	A	H	I	S	G	Y	J	R
13				F						
7		.		R						
11				A	N	D	Y			
19	J	E	A	N		O		S		
14				C		C	A	T		
22	D			E		T		U		
28	O					O		D		
30	G	I	R	L	F	R	I	E	N	D
5								N		
16			C	O	M	P	U	T	E	R

Ask Student A questions and find nine words in this grid, e.g. *What's the letter in B–16 ?*

	F	R	N	O	X	K	B	U	Q	Y
15										
10										
9										
21										
24										
16										
27										
8										
29										
3										

5.1 Find someone who . . .

Aim

To find classmates who like and dislike things

Language

Do you like . . . ?

Yes, I do. / No, I don't.

Skills

Speaking

Lesson link

Use after *Things I like* SB p33

Materials

One copy of the worksheet per student

Pre-activity (10 minutes)

- Write the following words on the board: *dogs, cats, dancing, cooking, pop music, classical music.* Point to each word and encourage students to ask you: *Do you like dogs? Do you like cooking?* etc. Each time, smile or frown and answer: *Yes, I do,* or *No, I don't.*

- Drill the question and answer forms with the class. Make sure students use rising intonation with the questions and falling intonation with the short answers.

- Invite students to ask their classmates similar questions. You may like to set up a chain where the student who answers a question then asks another student a question.

Procedure (20 minutes)

- Explain that students are going to ask each other about things they like and don't like.

- Give each student a copy of the worksheet. Give students time to read it and to check any items of vocabulary.

- Students mingle taking it in turns to ask and answer questions to complete their questionnaires with the names of students who like or don't like each item. Tell students that they can only ask each other one question at a time and then they must find a new partner (but if they meet each other again they can ask each other another question). Go around listening, making sure students are asking and answering the questions correctly.

- The first student to complete the questionnaire by filling both sections for each item with names wins. (It may not be possible for students to complete both sections for each item, in which case stop the activity after an appropriate time and declare the person with the most names the winner.)

Extension (10 minutes)

- Divide students into pairs. Ask students to guess what their partner likes and doesn't like and then complete the questionnaire for their partner with a tick (✔) or a cross (✘) for each item.

- Then students take it in turns to ask their partner questions to check their guesses. Go around listening, helping and correcting as necessary.

Find someone who ...

hamburgers

☺ _____

☹ _____

spaghetti

☺ _____

☹ _____

football

☺ _____

☹ _____

coffee

☺ _____

☹ _____

tea

☺ _____

☹ _____

cola

☺ _____

☹ _____

cats

☺ _____

☹ _____

dogs

☺ _____

☹ _____

cooking

☺ _____

☹ _____

dancing

☺ _____

☹ _____

pop music

☺ _____

☹ _____

classical music

☺ _____

☹ _____

5.2

Aim

To talk about prices

Language

How much is a . . .?
Prices

Skills

Speaking

Lesson link

Use after *Numbers and prices* SB p39

Materials

One copy of the worksheet per pair of students. Objects from magazines or catalogues with the price in pounds and pence written on the back and pieces of paper for the Extension

Answers

1	bag	£29.99
2	watch	£45.99
3	trainers	£80
4	mobile phone	£65
5	pint of beer	£2.30
6	magazine	£2.75
7	bar of chocolate	38p
8	camera	£125
9	TV	£299.99
10	CD	£12.99
11	computer	£800
12	pizza	£8.99

Pre-activity (5 minutes)

* Hold up your watch and ask (if you are in Great Britain): *How much is this watch in the shops?* (and if you are not) *How much is this watch in Great Britain?* (If you are not in Great Britain, make sure students know what the exchange rate is for pounds sterling.) Encourage students to be precise by using pounds and pence, e.g. *£55.99.* Write the suggested prices on the board, then tell the students what it actually cost and give the student who guessed most accurately a quick round of applause.

Procedure (20 minutes)

* Divide students into pairs and give each pair a copy of the worksheet. Tell students to match the words to the pictures. Then have a class feedback session.

* Then ask: *How much is the bag?* Tell students to look at the prices on the worksheet and choose the one they think matches the bag. Invite several students to tell you what they think it costs, encouraging them to say: *I think it is …*

* Now put pairs together to work in groups of four to six. Tell students to try to match the prices to the other objects. Point out that there are more prices on the worksheet than objects.

* When everyone has finished, have a class feedback session. The group who correctly matched the most prices to objects wins.

Extension (20 minutes)

* Explain that students are going to guess the prices of more objects. Give each student a piece of paper and make sure that everybody has a pen.

* Hold up a picture and ask: *How much is this (bag) in the shops?*

* Students write down how much they think it costs, without talking or showing their prices to each other at this stage.

* Then students mingle saying the price they wrote, and arrange themselves in order of price, increasing from left to right.

* When the line is ready, walk along the line asking each student in turn to say his/her price. When you reach the end of the line, announce the winner, i.e. the student who has guessed nearest to the price, and tell the class the correct price. Give the winner a quick round of applause.

* Repeat the procedure with the other pictures.

bag   beer   camera   CD   chocolate   computer   magazine   mobile phone
pizza   television   trainers   watch

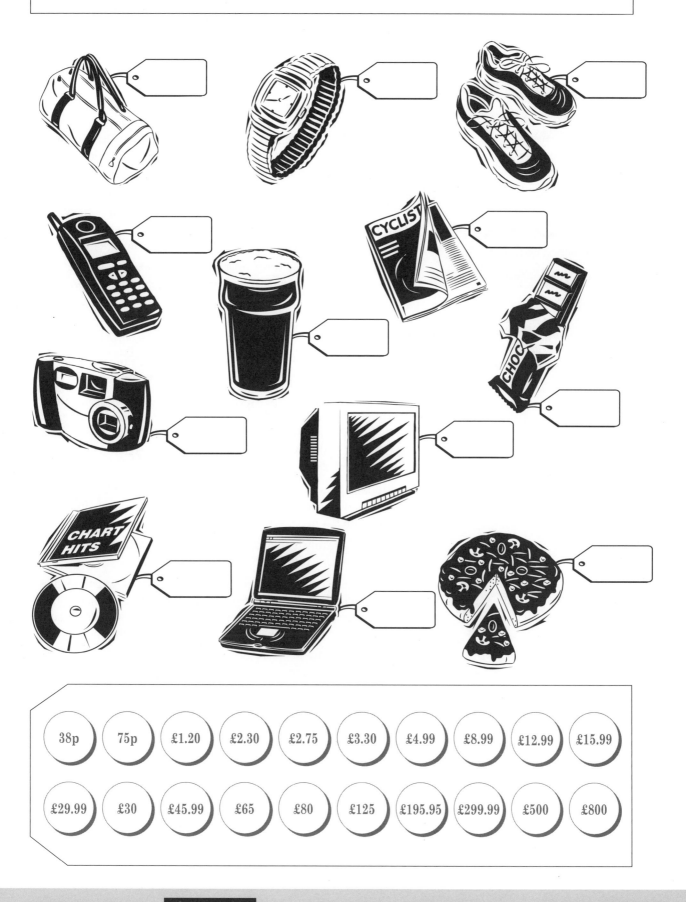

6.1

What time is it in . . .?

Aims

To find out the time in different cities

To solve time-zone puzzles

Language

The time

What time is it?

Skills

Speaking, Listening, and Reading

Lesson link

Use after *Starter* SB p40

Materials

One copy of the worksheet cut up per pair of students. A map of the world (optional)

Pre-activity (10 minutes)

- Write the following cities on the board: *Bangkok, Beijing, Budapest, Johannesburg, London, Los Angeles, Madrid, Moscow, New York, Rio de Janeiro, Singapore, Sydney, Tokyo.* Practise the pronunciation of the cities and if necessary, show students where the cities are on a map of the world.

- If you are teaching a mixed nationality class, ask two or three students: *What time is it? What time is it in your country now?* If you are teaching a monolingual group, find out if any of the students know what the time is in London or any other major city.

- Write the following times on the board: *4 a.m., 8 p.m.* Make sure students understand what *a.m.* and *p.m.* mean (*in the morning, in the afternoon/evening*).

Procedure (20 minutes)

- Explain that students are going to find out the time in cities around the world when it is twelve o'clock in London.

- Divide students into pairs. Give Students A worksheet A, and Students B worksheet B. Tell students not to show each other their worksheets. Give students time to read the worksheet and try to fill in the missing times using their general knowledge and/or guessing.

- Students now take it in turns to ask and answer questions about the cities: *What time is it in …?* Go around listening, helping and correcting as necessary.

- When pairs finish, they check their worksheets together, correcting any mistakes.

- Give pairs a copy of worksheet C. Allow students time to read it and to check any items of vocabulary. Work though the first time-zone puzzle with the class, making sure everybody understands what to do. Then ask pairs to work though the other puzzles. Go around helping as necessary.

- Check the answers with the class.

  Answers

1	12.30 a.m.	**3**	2 p.m.
2	12.10 p.m.	**4**	10.45 p.m.

Extension (10 minutes)

- Students, in their pairs, make up new time-zone puzzles for other pairs to solve.

A

Sheena's day

Sheena is an editor. She works

_____ (Where ...?) in Budapest.

She lives in the centre of town. She gets up at

_____ (When ...?) and she has tea

and toast for breakfast. At _____

(When ...?) she leaves home and she gets to work at

eight o'clock. In the morning she works

_____ (Where ...?). Then she has

lunch at twelve o'clock. For lunch, she usually has

_____ (What ...?) in an Italian restaurant. In the afternoon she works

_____ (Where ...?). She stops work at five o'clock. After work she goes

_____ (Where ...?) for an hour. She usually gets home at seven o'clock.

In the evening she likes to play _____ (What ...?). Then she makes a

sandwich for supper. After supper she watches _____ (What ...?) or

reads a book. She usually goes to bed at half past ten.

B

Sheena's day

Sheena is an editor. She works in a newspaper office in

Budapest. She lives in _____

(Where ...?). She gets up at seven o'clock and she has

_____ (What ...?) for breakfast.

At half past seven she leaves home and she gets to work

at _____ (When ...?). In the

morning she works in the office. Then she has lunch at

_____ (When ...?). For lunch,

she usually has pizza and ice-cream in

_____ (Where ...?). In the afternoon she works in a television studio.

She stops work at _____ (When ...?). After work she goes to the park

for an hour. She usually gets home at _____ (When ...?). In the

evening she likes to play tennis. Then she makes a _____ (What ...?)

for supper. After supper she watches the news on television or reads a book. She usually

goes to bed at _____ (When ...?).

7.1

Aim

To find out about each other's personal routines

Language

Present Simple questions

Skills

Speaking

Lesson link

Use after *I love it here* SB p48 & 49

Materials

One copy of the worksheet cut in half per pair of students

Question words

(Students A and B have the same questions but in a different order.)

What – have for breakfast?
Who – your favourite pop group?
What – do in the evening?
When/What time – go to bed?
When/What time – get up?
Who – your best friend?
What – drink in the morning?
Where – live?
When/Where – have lunch?
When/Where – go on holiday?
What – watch on television?
When/Where – have dinner?

Pre-activity (10 minutes)

- Elicit question words (*Where, When, Who, What*) and a 'typical' answer for each and write them on the board, e.g. *Where …? (At school / In the kitchen / Near the park), When …? (At ten o'clock / Today), Who …? (Sophie / Jacob), What …? (English / A pen / Tea).*

- Elicit the full questions forms for the 'typical' answers and write them on the board, e.g. *Where do you work? When do you get up? Who is your boyfriend? What do you have for breakfast?*, etc.

Procedure (20 minutes)

- Explain that students are going to ask each other questions to find out about their personal routines and lifestyles.

- Divide students into pairs. Give Students A worksheet A, and Students B worksheet B. Give students time to read through it and to check any items of vocabulary.

- Ask students to write a question word *Where, When, Who,* or *What,* (not the full question) in the gaps for each question. Tell students that in some cases two question words are possible and that they should choose one. (You may like to pair Students A and Students B during this stage.) Go around helping and correcting as necessary.

- Invite individual students to ask you some of the questions. Make sure the question form is correct, and then answer the question as naturally as the language level will allow.

- In their pairs, students take it in turns to interview each other. Tell students to make short notes on their partner's answers. Go around listening, helping and correcting as necessary.

- Have a class feedback session. Invite students to tell the class anything interesting they found out about their partner.

Extension (15 minutes)

- Students change partners, and interview each other about their previous partners. Encourage students to use full answers to practise the third person *s*, e.g.

Student A   *What time does Marta get up?*
Student B   *She gets up at seven o'clock.*

A

Question Word

▼ **Your partner's answers** ▼

have for breakfast **?**	_____
your favourite pop group **?**	_____
do in the evening **?**	_____
go to bed **?**	_____
get up **?**	_____
your best friend **?**	_____
drink in the morning **?**	_____
live **?**	_____
have lunch **?**	_____
go on holiday **?**	_____
watch on television **?**	_____
have dinner **?**	_____

✂ --

B

Question Word

▼ **Your partner's answers** ▼

drink in the morning **?**	_____
get up **?**	_____
go on holiday **?**	_____
go to bed **?**	_____
have dinner **?**	_____
have for breakfast **?**	_____
have lunch **?**	_____
your favourite pop group **?**	_____
live **?**	_____
your best friend **?**	_____
watch on television **?**	_____
do in the evening **?**	_____

7.2

Do you have a pen?

Aim

To play a card game by guessing noun–adjective combinations

Language

Do you have . . . ?
Adjectives

Skills

Speaking

Lesson link

Use after *Adjectives* SB p52

Materials

One copy of the worksheet cut up into cards per group of four students. Two blank cards per student and dictionaries for the Extension

Pre-activity (5 minutes)

- Revise the following questions and short answers forms by asking the students some simple questions, e.g. *Do you have a car? (Yes, I do. / No, I don't.) Is it a blue car?(Yes, it is. / No, it isn't.)*.

- Revise adjectives with the students. Call out an adjective and encourage students to call out the opposite, e.g. *cold – hot, lovely – horrible, big – small, expensive – cheap, new – old*, etc.

Procedure (20 minutes)

- Divide students into groups of four and give each group a set of picture cards and adjective word cards. Give students time to look at the cards and to check any items of vocabulary.

- Show the students the picture of the mobile phone, and hold up the adjective card *hot*. Ask the students if the two cards go together. Encourage students to find other strange or illogical combinations.

- Keeping the adjective and picture cards separate, groups turn the cards face down on the table. Students take it in turns to pick up a picture card and an adjective card without showing the rest of the group. If the student thinks the adjective–noun combination is too illogical, the student can exchange one of the cards for another. The other students in the group take it in turns to ask questions to guess the adjective–noun pair, e.g.

Student B	*Do you have a pen?*
Student A	*No, I don't.*
Student D	*Do you have a dictionary?*
Student A	*Yes, I do.*
Student C	*Is a big dictionary?*
Student A	*No, it isn't.*
Student B	*Is it a small dictionary?*
Student A	*Yes, it is.*

- The first student to guess the combination wins the cards. Go around listening, helping and correcting as necessary. Students play until all the cards are finished and the student with the most cards wins.

Extension (20 minutes)

- Give each student two blank cards. Ask students to draw a picture on one card and an adjective on the other. Students can work in their groups to do this, helping each other and looking up new words in a dictionary.

- Groups play again combining the new cards with the original set.

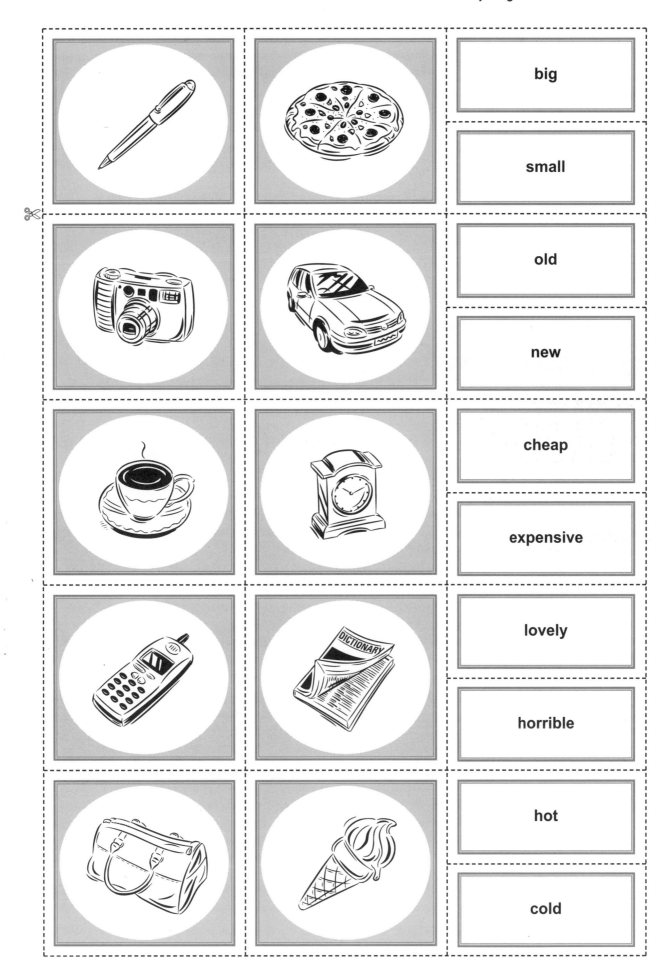

		big
		small
		old
		new
		cheap
		expensive
		lovely
		horrible
		hot
		cold

7.3

Hot and cold

Pre-activity (5 minutes)

- Revise some of the adjectives already familiar to the students by asking: *What's the opposite of 'hot'?* Elicit the answer *cold*, then ask: *How do you spell it, please?* and write it on the board as students dictate the letters to you. Repeat this for other adjectives, e.g. *What's the opposite of 'big'? (small) 'old'? (new)*, etc.

Procedure (15 minutes)

- Explain that students are going to find the opposites of adjectives.

- Divide students into pairs. Give Students A worksheet A, and Students B worksheet B. Tell students not to show each other their worksheets. Give students time to look at their worksheets, to check any items of vocabulary, and to practise saying the words using the phonetics to help them.

- In their pairs, students take it in turns to ask: *What's the opposite of …? How do you spell it, please?* and write in the missing adjectives on their worksheet. Go around listening, helping with pronunciation as necessary.

- When everybody has finished, check the answers with the class.

Extension (20 minutes)

- Divide students into groups of four students and give each group at least one dictionary and several pieces of paper and scissors.

- Ask students to look through the dictionaries and find adjective pairs that they like. The 'artists' from the group quickly sketch pictures illustrating each adjective, one sketch per piece of paper. Another student writes down the adjectives on a second piece of paper and the phonetics on a third piece of paper.

- When each group has found three or four adjective pairs, swap all the pieces of paper between the groups.

- Each group now tries to match the pictures, words, and phonetics for the adjective pairs.

- When groups have finished, they can ask the original group: *What's the opposite of …?* to see if they can remember!

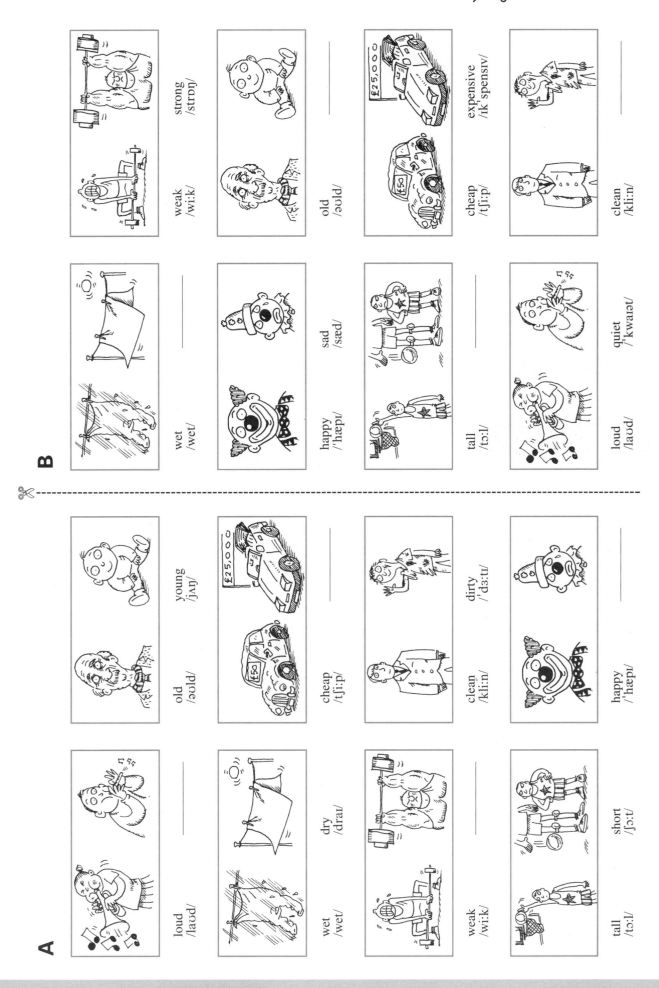

B

strong /strɒŋ/ — weak /wiːk/

old /əʊld/ —

expensive /ɪkˈspensɪv/ — cheap /tʃiːp/

clean /kliːn/ —

wet /wet/ —

happy /ˈhæpɪ/ — sad /sæs/

tall /tɔːl/ —

loud /laʊd/ — quiet /ˈkwaɪət/

✂ -

A

loud /laʊd/ —

old /əʊld/ — young /jʌŋ/

wet /wet/ —

cheap /tʃiːp/ —

dry /draɪ/ —

clean /kliːn/ — dirty /ˈdɜːtɪ/

weak /wiːk/ —

tall /tɔːl/ — short /ʃɔːt/

happy /ˈhæpɪ/ —

8.1

Find the gold

Pre-activity (5 minutes)

- Before the class, hide two 'gold bars' (e.g. two bars of chocolate) somewhere in the room. Show the students a similar object and tell them it is a gold bar. Tell the students that somewhere in the classroom there are two gold bars, and they can find out where they are by asking you questions, e.g. *Is there a gold bar in your bag?, Is there a gold bar under Marina's chair?* Each time, invite a student to look in the place suggested until the bars of gold are found. You could help the students by saying *warm* or *cold* each time they ask.

Procedure (20 minutes)

- Divide students into pairs. Give Students A worksheet A, and Students B worksheet B. Give students time to look at the picture of the house and to check any items of vocabulary. (You may like to revise rooms vocabulary at this point by asking students about where certain things are in the house, e.g. *Where's the computer?* (*It's in the bedroom.*), etc.

- Tell students to hide six 'gold bars' in the house without letting their partner see.

- Explain that students are going to try to find the gold bars in their partner's house. (Optional: You might like to tell students that they are burglars in the house. The problem is that they set off the burglar alarm and now only have three minutes before the police arrive.)

- Student A starts and has three minutes try to find the gold bars in Student B's house asking, e.g. *Are there any gold bars in the kitchen? Is there a gold bar in the fridge?* etc. Go around listening, helping and correcting as necessary. After three minutes shout: *Stop!* Then students swap roles and Student B has three minutes to find the gold bars in Student A's house. Go around listening, as before.

Extension (20 minutes)

- Students each write a brief description of their pictures describing where the gold bars were hidden, e.g. *There are two gold bars in the kitchen. There's a gold bar behind the fridge and there's a gold bar in the cupboard,* etc. Go around helping as necessary.

- When everybody has finished, collect all the descriptions and all the pictures of the houses. Put all the pictures around the room, and hand out the descriptions at random. Students read the description and try to find the picture it belongs to.

Aim

To find gold bars hidden in a house

Language

Is/Are there...?
Prepositions
Rooms and furniture

Skills

Speaking

Lesson link

Use after *Nicole's bedroom* SB p58

Materials

One copy of the worksheet cut in half per pair of students

A

✂ ---

B

8.2

Aims
To ask for and give directions
To solve a puzzle by following directions

Language
Directions

Skills
Speaking, Listening, and Reading

Lesson link
Use after *Directions* SB p63

Materials
One copy of the worksheet cut up per group of eight students

Pre-activity (5 minutes)

- Ask students about places near to the school, e.g. *Is there a bank near here?* Help students with the directions, making sure they begin: *Go out of the school, turn left/right.*

- Encourage students to ask you a similar question, and model the answer: *I'm sorry, I don't know. I don't come from here.*

Procedure (30 minutes)

- Explain that students are on holiday in a new town, and they are now all in the railway station. They are going to ask each other direction to places in the town.

- Divide students into groups of eight. Give Students A map A, Students B map B, and so on. Tell students not to show each other their maps. (If you have less than eight students in a group, give strong students more then one map.)

- In their groups, students approach each other and ask for directions to one of the places on their list e.g. *Is there a bank near here?* The student gives directions if he/she knows where it is, starting: *Go out of the railway station. Turn left/right,* or says: *I'm sorry, I don't know. I don't come from here.* Each time a student is given directions to a place, he/she writes the location on the map. Go around listening, helping and correcting as necessary.

- When everybody has finished, have a class feedback session and check the directions with the class. Draw the map on the board and ask individual students to give you directions to each place.

- Now explain that students were at the theatre and had problems finding their way home. Give each student a copy of the route they took. Tell them to put up their hand as soon as they work out where the hotel is but not to say anything. Each time a student puts up his/her hand, check that he/she has found the correct location.

- When most students have put up their hand, check the answer with the class. (The hotel is next to the theatre on the right!)

Extension (20 minutes)

- In pairs, students make up similar puzzles for each other. Students take it in turns to dictate a path for the other to follow, e.g. *Start at the bank. Go out of the bank, turn left, turn left, turn right. Where are you? (At the supermarket.).*

A

Ask for directions to the:

bus station   post office
theatre   chemist
supermarket   Internet café
newsagent

B

Ask for directions to the:

post office   bus station
Internet café   bank
chemist   newsagent
supermarket

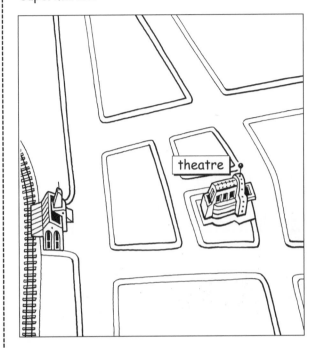

C

Ask for directions to the:

Internet café   post office
theatre   bank
bus station   supermarket
chemist

D

Ask for directions to the:

bank   bus station
post office   newsagent
theatre   chemist
Internet café

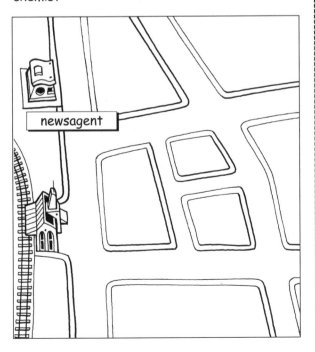

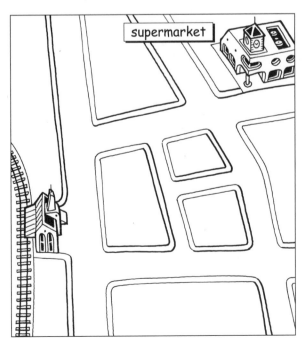

E

Ask for directions to the:

post office	supermarket
theatre	bank
bus station	newsagent
chemist	

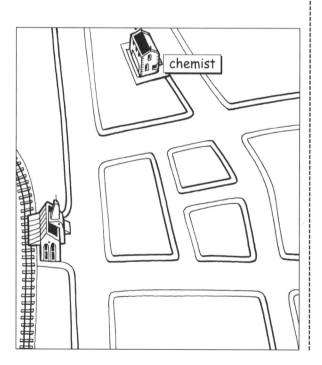

F

Ask for directions to the:

post office	supermarket
theatre	bank
newsagent	chemist
Internet café	

G

Ask for directions to the:

post office	supermarket
theatre	bank
bus station	newsagent
Internet café	

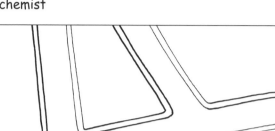

H

Ask for directions to the:

supermarket	theatre
bank	bus station
chemist	newsagent
Internet café	

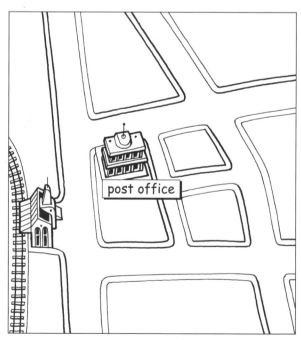

After the theatre you have some problems getting to your hotel. This is your route:

Go out of the theatre and turn left. Turn left and turn left again. Then turn right and turn right again. Go into the building on your left, come out again and turn left. Turn right and go straight on and straight on. Go into the building on your left and get something to eat. Then come out and turn right. Turn left and go straight on. Go into the building on your right and ask for directions. Come out, turn right and your hotel is on your right.

Where is your hotel?

After the theatre you have some problems getting to your hotel. This is your route:

Go out of the theatre and turn left. Turn left and turn left again. Then turn right and turn right again. Go into the building on your left, come out again and turn left. Turn right and go straight on and straight on. Go into the building on your left and get something to eat. Then come out and turn right. Turn left and go straight on. Go into the building on your right and ask for directions. Come out, turn right and your hotel is on your right.

Where is your hotel?

After the theatre you have some problems getting to your hotel. This is your route:

Go out of the theatre and turn left. Turn left and turn left again. Then turn right and turn right again. Go into the building on your left, come out again and turn left. Turn right and go straight on and straight on. Go into the building on your left and get something to eat. Then come out and turn right. Turn left and go straight on. Go into the building on your right and ask for directions. Come out, turn right and your hotel is on your right.

Where is your hotel?

After the theatre you have some problems getting to your hotel. This is your route:

Go out of the theatre and turn left. Turn left and turn left again. Then turn right and turn right again. Go into the building on your left, come out again and turn left. Turn right and go straight on and straight on. Go into the building on your left and get something to eat. Then come out and turn right. Turn left and go straight on. Go into the building on your right and ask for directions. Come out, turn right and your hotel is on your right.

Where is your hotel?

After the theatre you have some problems getting to your hotel. This is your route:

Go out of the theatre and turn left. Turn left and turn left again. Then turn right and turn right again. Go into the building on your left, come out again and turn left. Turn right and go straight on and straight on. Go into the building on your left and get something to eat. Then come out and turn right. Turn left and go straight on. Go into the building on your right and ask for directions. Come out, turn right and your hotel is on your right.

Where is your hotel?

After the theatre you have some problems getting to your hotel. This is your route:

Go out of the theatre and turn left. Turn left and turn left again. Then turn right and turn right again. Go into the building on your left, come out again and turn left. Turn right and go straight on and straight on. Go into the building on your left and get something to eat. Then come out and turn right. Turn left and go straight on. Go into the building on your right and ask for directions. Come out, turn right and your hotel is on your right.

Where is your hotel?

After the theatre you have some problems getting to your hotel. This is your route:

Go out of the theatre and turn left. Turn left and turn left again. Then turn right and turn right again. Go into the building on your left, come out again and turn left. Turn right and go straight on and straight on. Go into the building on your left and get something to eat. Then come out and turn right. Turn left and go straight on. Go into the building on your right and ask for directions. Come out, turn right and your hotel is on your right.

Where is your hotel?

After the theatre you have some problems getting to your hotel. This is your route:

Go out of the theatre and turn left. Turn left and turn left again. Then turn right and turn right again. Go into the building on your left, come out again and turn left. Turn right and go straight on and straight on. Go into the building on your left and get something to eat. Then come out and turn right. Turn left and go straight on. Go into the building on your right and ask for directions. Come out, turn right and your hotel is on your right.

Where is your hotel?

9.1

Where were you?

Aim

To ask and answer about classmates' whereabouts last Saturday

Language

was/were

Skills

Speaking

Lesson link

Use after *Today and yesterday* SB p67

Materials

One copy of the worksheet cut up into cards per class of fifteen students

Pre-activity (10 minutes)

- Ask a student: *Where were you at ten o'clock on Saturday morning?* Then ask another student about the student you have just asked: *Pedro, where was Maria at ten o'clock on Saturday morning?* Then ask other students about their whereabouts at other times on Saturday morning, afternoon, evening, and night.

- Then set up a chain round the class with a student asking the person on his/her right, e.g. *Where were you at …?* and then asking the student on his/her left: *Where was Jack at …?*, etc. Make sure students use the right prepositions, e.g. *at home, at school, on a bus, in a car, in bed*, etc.

Procedure (25 minutes)

- Explain that students are going to ask each other about their whereabouts last Saturday.

- Ask students to write the names of everybody in the class on a piece of paper. Then give each student a different time card. (If you have a large class, divide students into two groups.)

- Students mingle taking it in turns to ask each other where they were at the time on their card. After each conversation they go back to their desks and write the answer next to the name of the student they spoke to. Go around listening, helping and correcting as necessary.

- When everybody has finished, divide students into pairs. In their pairs, students write a sentence describing where the other students were at the time on the two cards, e.g. *At ten o'clock, five students were at school, four were at work, and one was at home.* Go around helping as necessary.

- Have a class feedback session to check the accuracy of some of the sentences. Invite several students to read out their sentences and then ask the class: *Who was at school at ten o'clock?* (five students should put up their hands).

Extension (10 minutes)

- Collect everybody's sentences and display them as a class profile of last Saturday. Give students time to read everybody's sentences.

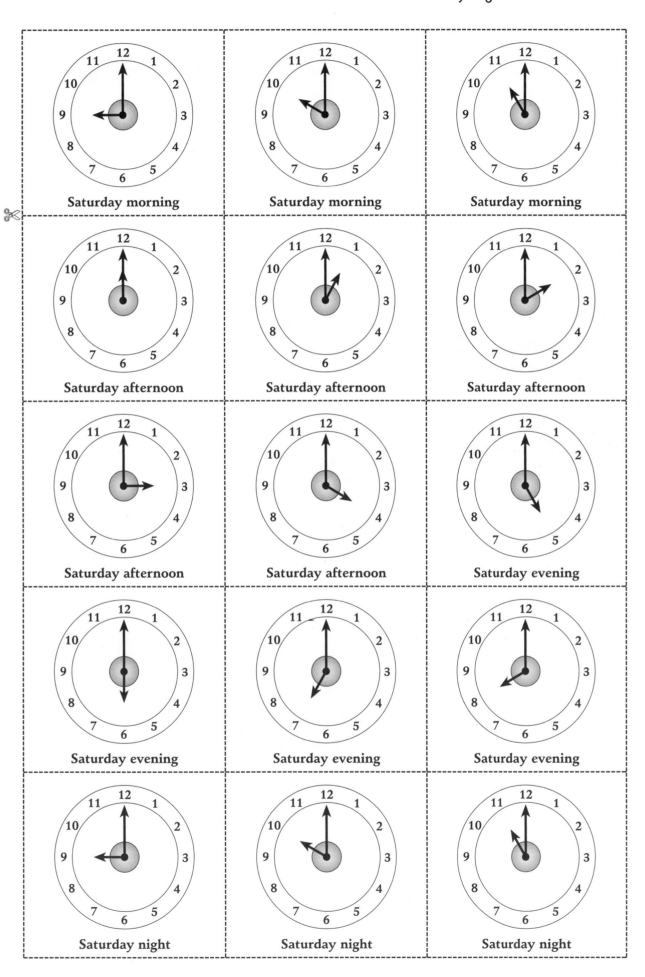

9.2

Sorry I'm late!

Aim

To play a board game to make excuses for being late or early for a party

Language

Past Simple

Skills

Speaking and Writing

Lesson link

Use after *Vocabulary and Reading* SB p68 & 69

Materials

One copy of the worksheet cut up into cards and the board game per group of four students. Each student needs a counter and each group needs a die

Pre-activity (10 minutes)

- Teach/Elicit the past tense forms (and meaning, if necessary) of the following verbs: *talk (talked), take (took), is/are (was/were), buy (bought), watch (watched), go (went), have (had), write (wrote), run (ran), look (looked), take (took).*

- Call out a present tense verb. Students tell you the past tense form. Call out a past tense form. Students tell you the present tense form.

Procedure (25 minutes)

- Explain that students are going to play a board game about getting to a party where they are either late or too early. Pre-teach *Go forward, Go back*, and *Miss a turn.*

- Divide students into groups of four and give each group a copy of the board game and a set of cards placed face down on the table.

- Students place their counters on the *Leave home* square and then take it in turns to throw the die, moving the corresponding number of places along the board. When a student lands on a square with *Sorry!*, the student to his/her left takes a card from the pile and reads it aloud, e.g. *You talk to a friend. Miss a turn.* The playing student changes the sentence into its past tense form to make an excuse for being late, e.g. *Sorry I'm late. I talked to a friend.* The student then writes the sentence in his/her notebook. He/She also misses a turn next go. If the card is a "go forward" card, the student apologises for arriving early, e.g. *You take a train. Go forward three places.* The playing student changes it into its past tense form to make an excuse for being early, e.g. *Sorry I'm early. I took a train.* The student then writes the sentence in his/her notebook and moves forward three places. Go around listening, helping and correcting as necessary.

- When all the cards have been used, shuffle them and keep playing. The game continues until most or all students have arrived at the party.

Extension (10 minutes)

- Divide students into pairs to talk about what they did on the way to the party. Model the conversation with a strong student first, e.g.
  Teacher   *On the way to the party, I bought a present.*
  Student   *On the way to the party, I talked to a friend.*
  Teacher   *Really? I talked to a friend, too. And I had two beers.*
  Student   *Oh, I had three coffees in a bar.*

You talk to a friend.
Miss a turn.

A friend takes you in his car.
Go forward three places.

The bus is late.
Go back three places.

You buy a present.
Go back two places.

You watch a football match
on TV in a shop.
Go back two places.

You go by taxi.
Go forward three places.

You have a coffee in a café.
Miss a turn.

You go by bus.
Go forward two places.

You have a beer in a bar.
Miss a turn.

You write an e-mail
to a friend in an Internet café.
Go back three places.

You run for one kilometre.
Go forward two places.

You go the wrong way.
Miss a turn.

You look at a beautiful
painting in a shop.
Go back two places.

You take a train.
Go forward three places.

You are early!
Go forward two places.

You have something to eat.
Miss a turn.

9.3

Aim

To find words hidden in a grid of letters

Language

Ordinal numbers
The alphabet
Work and freetime vocabulary

Skills

Speaking and Listening

Lesson link

Use after *When's your birthday?* SB p70 & 71

Materials

One copy of the worksheet cut in half per pair of students

Answers

Worksheet A

A	D	E	W	R	I	T	E	R	O	N	L
W	R	A	S	P	E	C	U	T	J	M	I
P	B	R	T	S	M	H	D	O	O	Y	
I	X	A	L	F	U	P	E	A	D	E	B
N	C	O	F	S	I	S	C	E	T	M	R
T	H	O	Q	K	R	L	E	H	R	A	R
E	E	I	M	U	S	I	C	I	A	N	E
R	M	I	N	P	L	I	C	E	M	A	W
N	I	G	S	T	U	D	I	O	T	G	I
E	S	I	T	O	R	T	E	A	C	E	H
T	T	A	D	O	C	T	E	A	S	R	E
D	O	I	R	E	C	T	O	R	I	N	T

1 THEATRE   2 CINEMA   3 BOOK   4 SAILING
5 RESTAURANT   6 HOTEL   7 SKIING
8 TENNIS   9 BEACH   10 OPERA   11 WEATHER

Worksheet B

F	R	E	I	D	A	S	O	C	D	R	O
T	H	E	A	T	R	E	N	I	L	Y	K
E	K	A	S	A	I	L	I	N	G	I	G
A	W	A	K	T	O	P	L	E	Y	Q	W
N	E	M	I	S	A	P	R	M	G	H	I
I	A	M	I	N	T	U	E	A	W	E	L
N	T	A	N	N	I	S	R	R	E	H	S
G	H	O	G	L	K	I	S	A	A	I	N
H	E	T	L	O	F	U	T	Y	N	B	O
A	R	H	O	T	E	L	E	N	G	T	H
O	S	B	E	A	C	H	Y	R	E	E	D
T	E	L	V	I	S	T	O	N	S	E	I

1 INTERNET   2 WRITER   3 MUSICIAN
4 NURSE   5 DIRECTOR   6 OFFICE   7 JOB
8 CHEMIST   9 COMPUTER   10 STUDIO
11 MANAGER

Pre-activity (5 minutes)

- Choose a word the students know, e.g. *English,* and draw the corresponding number of letter lines (7) on the board. Now tell the students: *The third letter is 'G',* and get a student to come forward and write *G* on the corresponding line. Ask the students to try and guess the word. If no-one guesses the word, give the students another clue, e.g. *The sixth letter is 'S',* and so on until someone guesses the word.

Procedure (20 minutes)

- Explain that students are going to help each other find words hidden in word grids.

- Divide students into pairs. Give Students A worksheet A, and Students B worksheet B. Tell students that Students A are looking for words connected with work and Students B are looking for word connected with freetime. Explain that the words can go across →, down ↓, diagonally up ↗ or diagonally down ↘. Drill these words and then write them on the board for students to refer to later.

- Explain or model how to play with a strong student. In pairs, students tell each other the first clue. Student A says: *First word. Seven letters across. The second letter is 'H'.* Student B says: *First word. Seven letters down. The fourth letter is 'E'.* Encourage students to take notes for the clues in case they forget any details.

- Both students then look for the word in their grid. The first student to find the word shouts *Stop!* The other student now stops searching, and the first student dictates the word, letter by letter, to his/her partner who writes it down in the spaces. If the word is correct and fits the number of spaces, the students then move on to the second word. (The pair do not wait for both students to find the words.) If the word is wrong, the second student can have a further thirty seconds to try to find his/her word. If he/she doesn't manage to find the word in that time, the pair move on to the next word. Go around listening and helping as necessary.

- The game continues until all the words have been searched for (but not necessarily found). The winner is the student who has correctly found most words and dictated them to his/her partner. When students have reached this stage, let them check their grids together and find any words they weren't able to find before.

Extension (20 minutes)

- In pairs, students can make their own word search grids to swap with another pair.

A Work word search

Tell Student B the clue for his/her word, e.g. *First word. Seven letters across. The second letter is 'H'.* Then listen to Student B's clue for your word, e.g. *First word. Eight letters down. The fourth letter is 'E'.* Then try to find the word in your grid (*Internet*).

A	D	E	W	R	I	T	E	R	O	N	L
W	R	A	S	P	E	C	U	T	J	M	I
P	B	R	T	S	I	M	H	D	O	O	Y
I	X	A	L	F	U	P	E	A	D	E	B
N	C	O	F	S	I	S	C	E	T	M	R
T	H	O	Q	K	R	L	E	H	R	A	R
E	E	I	M	U	S	I	C	I	A	N	E
R	M	I	N	P	L	I	C	E	M	A	W
N	I	G	S	T	U	D	I	O	T	G	I
E	S	I	T	O	R	T	E	A	C	E	H
T	T	A	D	O	C	T	E	A	S	R	E
D	D	I	R	E	C	T	O	R	I	N	T

Clues for Student B:

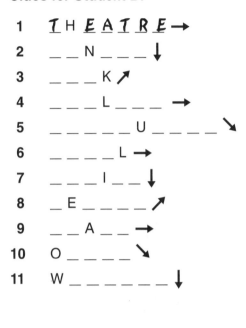

1 T H E A T R E →
2 _ _ N _ _ _ _ ↓
3 _ _ _ K ↗
4 _ _ _ L _ _ _ →
5 _ _ _ _ _ _ U _ _ _ _ ↘
6 _ _ _ _ L →
7 _ _ _ I _ _ ↓
8 _ E _ _ _ _ _ ↗
9 _ _ A _ _ →
10 O _ _ _ _ ↘
11 W _ _ _ _ _ _ ↓

B Freetime word search

Listen to Student A's clue for your word, e.g. *First word. Seven letters across. The second letter is 'H'.* Then tell Student A the clues for his/her word, e.g. *First word. Eight letters down. The fourth letter is 'E'.* Then try to find the word in your grid (*theatre*).

F	R	E	I	D	A	S	O	C	D	R	O
T	H	E	A	T	R	E	N	I	L	Y	K
E	K	A	S	A	I	L	I	N	G	I	G
A	W	A	K	T	O	P	L	E	Y	Q	W
N	E	M	I	S	A	P	R	M	G	H	I
I	A	M	I	N	T	U	E	A	W	E	L
N	T	A	N	N	I	S	R	R	E	H	S
G	H	O	G	L	K	I	S	A	A	I	N
H	E	T	L	O	F	U	T	Y	N	B	O
A	R	H	O	T	E	L	E	N	G	T	H
O	S	B	E	A	C	H	E	R	E	E	D
T	E	L	V	I	S	T	O	N	S	E	I

Clues for Student A:

1 I N T E R N E T ↓
2 W _ _ _ _ _ _ →
3 _ _ _ _ _ _ _ A _ →
4 _ U _ _ _ ↗
5 _ _ _ _ _ _ _ _ R →
6 _ _ F _ _ _ ↗
7 _ _ B ↘
8 _ _ _ M _ _ _ ↓
9 _ _ _ P _ _ _ _ ↘
10 _ _ _ _ _ O →
11 _ _ _ _ G _ _ _ ↓

10.1

Aim

To write a story in the past tense

Language

Past Simple irregular verbs

Skills

Writing

Lesson link

Use after *Yesterday* SB p72 & 73

Materials

One copy of the worksheet cut up per pair of students

Suggested answers

d   Carlo gave Julia some flowers.
j   Carlo said "Please marry me."
c   They got married.
l   They flew to London.
a   They saw Big Ben.
g   Carlo took photographs in London.
b   They went to Paris.
f   Carlo sold his photographs.
i   They bought a house.
k   Carlo worked in an art gallery.
h   Julia taught French.
e   Julia and Carlo had a baby.

Other variations:

k, l, h, d, j, c, a, g, b, f, i, e
k, h, d, j, c, l, a, g, b, f, i, e
h, d, j, c, l, a, g, l, f, i, e, k

Pre-activity (5 minutes)

- Teach/Elicit the past tense forms (and meaning, if necessary) of the following verbs: *give (gave), get married (got married), fly (flew), see (saw), take (took), go (went), sell (sold), buy (bought), teach (taught), have (had), say (said).*

- Call out a present tense verb. Students tell you the past tense form. Call out a past tense form. Students tell you the present tense form.

Procedure (30 minutes)

- Write *A love story* on the board and make sure everybody understands what it means. Explain that students are going to put pictures in order to tell a love story about Carlo and Julia.

- Divide students into pairs and give each pair a jumbled set of picture cards. Give students time to discuss and predict the order of the story. Go around asking: *Which picture is first? Which picture is second?* Accept any suggestions but don't comment on whether the suggestions are right or wrong. Tell students that various options are possible. Tell students that the pictures are labelled a–l for identification and do not show the order.

- Write the following verbs on the board: *buy, fly, get married, give, go, have, say, see, sell, take, teach, work.* Ask students to match each verb with a picture.

- In their pairs, students now write the story using the verbs in the past tense. Go round helping with vocabulary as necessary. Encourage students to add details to make the story more interesting.

- Group two or three pairs together. Pairs take it in turns to tell their stories and compare the similarities and differences. Go around listening, helping and correcting as neccessary.

- Have a class feedback session.

Extension (10 minutes)

- Display all the stories on the classroom wall. Give students time to read each other's stories and try to find all the stories which have the events in the same order as their story.

10.2

Did you have a good holiday?

Aim
To ask and answer questions about holidays

Language
Past Simple questions
Irregular verbs
both

Skills
Speaking and Writing

Lesson link
Use after *Did you have a good weekend?* SB p74 & 75

Materials
One copy of worksheet cut in half per pair of students

Pre-activity (5 minutes)

- Introduce the topic of holidays by asking individual students: *Where did you go on holiday? What did you see? Where did you stay? What did you do?* etc.

- Encourage the students to ask you about your holiday. (The only new word in the worksheet is *mountain* so you may wish to include it in your answers about your holiday!)

Procedure (20 minutes)

- Explain that students are going to exchange information to find out about Aisha and Marco's holidays last summer.

- Divide students into pairs. Give Students A worksheet A, and Students B worksheet B. Give students time to read through it and to check any items of vocabulary.

- Demonstrate the activity by asking Students A: *Where did Marco go? (He went to Dublin in Ireland.)* Then ask Students B: *Where did Aisha go? (She went to Galway in Ireland.).* Make sure students understand that the questions are in a different order in the two worksheets.

- Write on the board: *Aisha and Marco both went to Ireland.* Make sure students understand the meaning of *both*.

- Ask students to interview each other to find out what other things both Aisha and Marco did. Go around listening, helping and correcting as necessary.

- When everybody has finished, have a class feedback session to discuss what they both did on their holidays.

> **Answers**
> Marco and Aisha both went to Ireland, stayed two weeks, stayed in a hotel, visited their English teacher, and had a good time.

Extension (20 minutes)

- Students now put away their worksheets and, in their pairs, write about Aisha and Marco, trying to remember as much as possible, e.g. *Aisha and Marco both went to Ireland, but Aisha went in August and Marco went in September,* etc.

- When everybody has finished, ask pairs to swap texts with another pair and check each other's work. If you like, students can give one point for each factually correct statement, and deduct a point for each incorrect statement.

A

MARCO

AISHA

Where / go?	Dublin, in Ireland	
When / go?	last September	
How long / stay?	two weeks	
What / do?	went to the theatre and cinema	
What / see?	many beautiful buildings	
How / travel?	by bus	
Who / visit?	his English teacher	
What / buy?	two presents	
Where / stay?	in an expensive hotel	
Have a good time?	yes – very good	

✂ --

B

MARCO

AISHA

When / go?		last August
Where / go?		Galway, in Ireland
What / buy?		a present
How long / stay?		two weeks
How / travel?		by train
What / do?		went for walks, went swimming
Where / stay?		in a cheap hotel
What / see?		the sea and mountains
Who / visit?		her English teacher
Have a good time?		yes – fantastic

Pre-activity (5 minutes)

- Ask individual students about their abilities, e.g. *Can you swim?*, etc. Make sure they answer correctly: *Yes, I can*, or *No, I can't.* Make sure students use rising intonation with the questions and falling intonation with the short answers.

- Invite students to ask their classmates similar questions. You may like to set up a chain where the student who answers a question then asks another student a question.

Procedure (10 minutes)

- Explain that students are going to ask each other about their abilities.

- Ask students to write the names of everybody in the class on a piece of paper. Then give each student a card. (If you have a large class, divide your students into two groups.)

- Students mingle and ask each other if they can do the activity on their card, e.g. *Can you ski? Yes, I can*, or *No, I can't.* Tell students not to write anything down at this stage. Go around listening, helping and correcting as necessary.

- After students have asked everybody in the class (or their group), ask them to go back to their desks. Give students one minute to try to put ticks by everyone who said: *Yes, I can.*

- Then students swap their list and the card with another student.

- Students mingle and check how well the first student remembered by asking everyone: *Can you . . . ?* according to the card they now have and the list of names.

- Have a class feedback session to find out how many people remembered everything correctly.

Extension (10 minutes)

- In small groups, students write sentences about the class, e.g. *Five people can play the piano. Nobody can ski.* All the sentences can be collated to form a class profile.

play the guitar?

ride a horse?

draw?

play chess?

speak two foreign languages?

swim 500 metres?

read music?

ride a motorbike?

run five kilometres?

ski?

cook pizza?

play the piano?

11.2

Yes, of course.

Aim

To ask and answer requests

Language

Can I/you...?

Yes, of course.

I'm sorry. I can't.

Skills

Speaking and Reading.

Lesson link

Use after *Request and offers* SB p83

Materials

One copy of the worksheet cut up into cards per group of four students

Pre-activity (5 minutes)

- Revise the language of requests and offers by asking individual students to do things, e.g. *Can you open the window, please? (Yes, of course.) Can I borrow your dictionary? (Sorry, I don't have one.),* etc.

Procedure (20 minutes)

- Explain that students are going to play a game where they make requests and try to find the student in their group who has the *Yes, of course* response to their request.

- Divide students into groups of four. Give Students A worksheet A, Students B worksheet B, and so on. (For groups of less than four students, give the strongest student two cards.) Tell students not to show each other their cards. Give students time to read their card and to check any items of vocabulary.

- Student A begins by asking one of the other three students in the group (B, C, or D) the first request at the top of his/her card: *Can I use your mobile phone, please?* Student B or D if asked replies: *I'm sorry, I left my phone at home,* but Student C if asked replies: *Yes, of course. My mobile phone is in my bag.*

- If the student answers: *Yes, of course ...* Student A can cross off that request. If the student answers: *I'm sorry ...* Student A has to wait until the next turn before asking the request again to another student in the group.

- After Student A has asked one request, it is then Student B's turn, then C's, and so on. The aim is to be the first to cross off all three requests, but the game should continue until all students have crossed off all their requests. Go around listening, helping and correcting as necessary.

Extension (15 minutes)

- Students cover the answer part of the cards and practise asking and answering the requests in their groups.

- Invite individual students to the front of the class to mime one of the requests. The class tries say what the request is. Then the student chooses another student to answer (with either a positive or negative response).

A

▶ **Can I use your mobile phone, please?**

▶ **Can you tell me the time, please?**

▶ **Can I borrow a pen, please?**

I'm sorry, I can't. My sister has my car.

I'm sorry, I don't have any coffee.

I'm sorry, I don't have time to help you at the moment.

Yes, of course. Where do you want me to put your bag?

Yes, of course. It's hot in here.

I'm sorry, but I'm very hot!

I'm sorry, it's my friend's chair.

I'm sorry, it's my brother's birthday party tonight.

I'm sorry, we don't make hamburgers here.

B

▶ **Can you drive me to the station, please?**

▶ **Can you open the window, please?**

▶ **Can I have a hamburger, please?**

I'm sorry, I can't. I don't have a watch.

Yes, of course. Do you want sugar in your coffee?

I'm sorry, it's my friend's chair.

I'm sorry, I don't have time to help you at the moment.

I'm sorry, I left my phone at home.

I'm sorry, I have lots of bags, too.

Yes, of course. What time does your party start?

I'm sorry, I don't have a pen.

Yes, of course. It's very cold in here!

C

▶ **Can I sit here, please?**

▶ **Can you take my bag, please?**

▶ **Can you help me, please?**

Yes, of course. My mobile phone is in my bag.

I'm sorry, I don't have any coffee.

I'm sorry, I don't have a pen.

I'm sorry, but I'm very hot!

Yes, of course. What time do you want to be at the station?

I'm sorry, it's my brother's birthday party tonight.

I'm sorry, but I'm very cold.

I'm sorry, I can't. I don't have a watch.

Yes, of course. Do you want a big or a small hamburger?

D

▶ **Can I close the window, please?**

▶ **Can I have a coffee, please?**

▶ **Can you come to my party tonight, please?**

I'm sorry, we don't make hamburgers here.

I'm sorry, but I'm very cold.

Yes, of course. Do you want a blue pen or a red pen?

Yes, of course. It's four o'clock.

Yes, of course. Please sit down.

I'm sorry, I can't. My sister has my car.

Yes, of course. How can I help?

I'm sorry, I left my phone at home.

I'm sorry, I have lots of bags, too.

12.1

Aim
To find out what other students would like to do
Language
Would you like to . . . ?
Yes, I would. / No, I wouldn't.
Skills
Speaking and Reading
Lesson link
Use after *Talking about you* SB p91
Materials
One copy of the worksheet per student

Pre-activity (10 minutes)

- Draw a picture of a man on the board with a thought bubble. In the thought bubble draw a picture of a Formula 1 racing car. Write the sentence, getting the students to help you complete it: *He would like to drive a Formula 1 car.*

- Ask: *Would you like to drive a Formula 1 car?* Drill the correct short answer form: *Yes, I would,* or *No, I wouldn't.*

- Rub out the car and draw a horse in the thought bubble. Elicit the sentence: *He would like to ride a horse.* Encourage students to ask you: *Would you like to ride a horse?*

- Continue rubbing out and drawing different pictures in the thought bubble. Elicit the sentence from one half of the class, the question from the other half, and the answer from individual students.

Procedure (20 minutes)

- Explain that students are going to look at a questionnaire and choose five things they would like to do, then interview their classmates to find out what they would like to do.

- Give each student a copy of the worksheet. Give students time to read through it, to check any items of vocabulary, and then to choose five things they would like to do.

- Students mingle, asking and telling each other about the things they would like to do, e.g. *What would you like to do?* Each time two students find they have chosen the same thing, they say: *I'd like to do that, too.* Go around listening, helping and correcting as necessary. (Alternatively, if you have a large class, students can work in small groups to find out what other students in the group would like to do.)

- When students have finished interviewing their classmates, have a class feedback session. Work through the list asking for a show of hands for each item to find the most (and least) popular choice.

Extension (15 minutes)

- Conduct a class survey. Assign a question to each student. Students mingle, asking everyone in the class their question and making notes. When everyone has finished, each student reports to the class his/her findings: *Five students would like to live in America and ten students wouldn't.*

Dreams

Tick (✔) five things you would like to do.

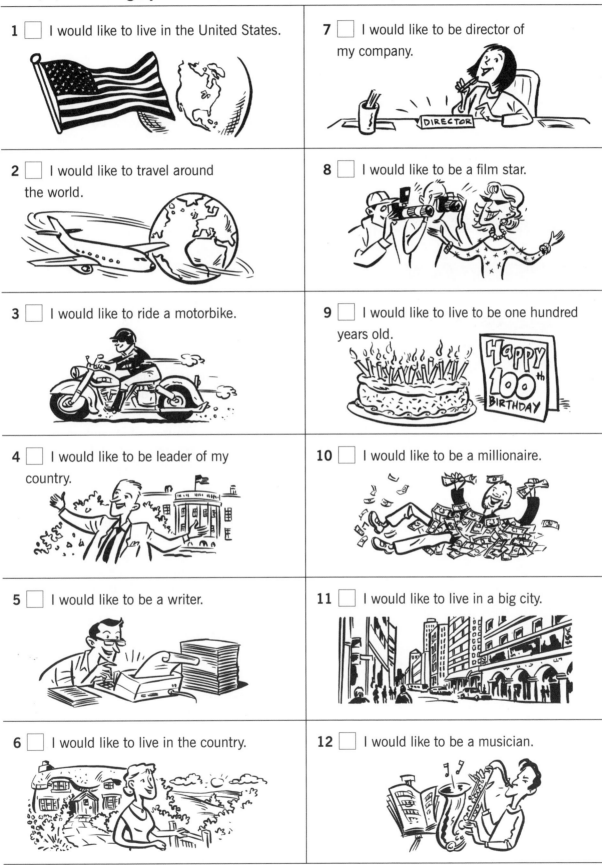

1 ☐ I would like to live in the United States.

2 ☐ I would like to travel around the world.

3 ☐ I would like to ride a motorbike.

4 ☐ I would like to be leader of my country.

5 ☐ I would like to be a writer.

6 ☐ I would like to live in the country.

7 ☐ I would like to be director of my company.

8 ☐ I would like to be a film star.

9 ☐ I would like to live to be one hundred years old.

10 ☐ I would like to be a millionaire.

11 ☐ I would like to live in a big city.

12 ☐ I would like to be a musician.

12.2

Aim
To play a game with picture cards of different dishes
Language
would like
Food
Skills
Speaking
Lesson link
Use after *In a restaurant* SB p92 & 93
Materials
One copy of the worksheet cut up into cards per group of four students

Pre-activity (10 minutes)

- Divide students into groups of four and give each group a set of the delicious food picture cards. Ask groups to divide the dishes into *starters, main courses,* and *desserts.* (*Starter: mixed salad, seafood cocktail, soup, cheese sandwich. Main course: roast chicken, steak and fries, pizza, hamburger. Dessert: chocolate cake, fruit, apple pie, ice-cream.*)

Procedure (20 minutes)

- Explain that students are going to play a game with delicious and disgusting food. Make sure students understand the meaning of *delicious* and *disgusting.*

- Ask students, on their own and in secret, to choose and write in their notebooks a three-course meal from the picture cards in the Pre-activity.

- Then give the same groups of four students a set of disgusting food picture cards. Tell students to mix the two sets of cards thoroughly and then deal the cards face down so that each student has six cards. Tell students not to show each other their cards.

- If a student is dealt a delicious picture card for an item on his/her list, he/she can quietly tick the item on the list and place the card face down in front of him/her, without telling the other students what the card is.

- In their groups, students take it in turns to ask another student for a dish from his/her chosen meal, e.g. Student A says to student C: *I would like the soup, please.* If Student C doesn't have a picture card of soup, he/she says: *I'm sorry. I don't have any soup.* If Student C has a picture card of soup (either delicious or disgusting) he/she gives Student A the card face down and says: *Certainly. Here you are.* Student A leaves the card face down on the table in front of him/her and ticks the soup off his/her meal list. Go around listening, helping and correcting as necessary.

- Because there are only two of any item, once a dish has been ticked off twice, any other student wishing to order it won't be able to and should cross it off his/her list. The game continues until all the dishes on the students meal lists have been either ticked or crossed off. The students then turn up all the cards in front of them and see how many delicious and how many disgusting dishes they collected. The winner in each group is the student with the most delicious dishes.

Extension (20 minutes)

- Using dictionaries, students write their own menus. This can be based on students' national dishes, favourite restaurants, etc.

Delicious   Disgusting

12.3

What would you like?

Pre-activity (15 minutes)

- Ask students about eating out in restaurants, e.g. *How often do you go to restaurants? When did you last go to a restaurant? Was the food good?* etc.

- Give each group a set of delicious food picture cards. Ask them to quickly write a menu with the dishes dividing them into starters, main dishes, and desserts. Tell students to add prices by each dish.

Procedure (30 minutes)

- Explain that students are going to practise ordering food in a restaurant.

- Divide students into groups of four and give each group a copy of the worksheet. Give the students time to put the two sections of the worksheet together to see how the flow chart works and to check any items of vocabulary.

- Ask students, in their groups, to develop a dialogue following the flow chart. Go round helping the students, making sure they are using polite English, e.g. *I would like … , Can I have …?*, etc. and helping with vocabulary as necessary.

- Ask students to practise the dialogues in their groups, taking it in turns to be the waiter.

- When everybody has played the role of the waiter, stop the activity and ask for one waiter from each group to join you at your desk with the waiter section of the worksheet. Give each waiter a pen and a piece of paper, the menu prepared in the Pre-activity, and a set of delicious and disgusting picture cards (which they leave on the teacher's table). The 'customers' stay in their groups around a table, with the customer flow chart on the table for all to see.

- The waiters now approach a table (but *not* their original groups) to take the group's order. When the waiters take an order, they should note what was ordered, go to the teacher's desk, and collect the 'food'. Tell them they can choose if they want to take a delicious dish or a disgusting dish. When they bring the food to the table, encourage the students to react to the food, e.g. *Mmm. This is delicious*, or *Ugh. This is horrible/disgusting!* Confident students can even say to the waiter: *Please take this back. I'd like another one.* Go around listening, helping and correcting as necessary.

- If there is time at the end, change waiters and ask groups to do the role play again.

Extension (15 minutes)

- In pairs, students write a dialogue based on the flow chart.

Waiter

Customer

> Bring the menu.
> Ask what drinks the customers would like.

> Order drinks.
> Read the menu.

> Go and get the drinks, and bring to the table.
> Ask what starter and main course the customers would like.

> Order the starter and main course.

> Make notes. Go and get the food, and bring it to the table.
> Take the menu.

> Thank the waiter. Eat!
> Is the food good or bad?

> Anything else?

> Ask for desserts and tea or coffee.

> Make notes. Go and get the desserts, and bring to the table. Go and get the coffees or teas, and bring to the table.

> Thank the waiter. Eat!
> Is the food good or bad?

> Anything else?

> Ask for the bill.

> Give the customers the bill.

Aim

To decide if statements about a picture are true or false

Language

Present Continuous

There is/are ...

Skills

Reading and Writing

Lesson link

Use after *Work and holidays* SB p97

Materials

One copy of the worksheet cut up per pair of students.

Answers

1 False. (There are two cars in the station car park.)
2 True.
3 False. (One person is eating a sandwich.)
4 True.
5 False. (A boy is buying an ice-cream in the café.
6 False. (A man and a woman are buying train tickets.)
7 True.
8 False. (The time is 10.15.)
9 True.
10 False. (A man is reading a newspaper.)
11 True.
12 False. (Two people are getting onto a train.)
13 False. (A man is taking a photograph on Platform 1.)
14 True.

Pre-activity (5 minutes)

- Ask the students to close their eyes. Make statements using the Present Continuous or *There is/are ...* about the classroom, or students in the room, e.g. *Marija is sitting next to Pedro. There's a blue clock on the wall.* Encourage students to say: *True* or *False* each time.

Procedure (15 minutes)

- Explain that students are going to look at a picture of a railway station for a few moments. Then they are going to mark statements about the picture true or false from memory.

- Divide students into pairs and give each pair a copy of the picture section (A) of the worksheet. Give students time to look at the picture and to check any items of vocabulary. Make sure students understand the meaning of *platform* and *tree*.

- Collect in the pictures and give each pair a copy of the statements section (B) of the worksheet. In their pairs, students mark the statements true or false.

- When they have finished, ask pairs to compare their answers with another pair. Then give the picture back to the pairs to check their answers.

- Have a class feedback session. Ask students to correct the false statements, e.g. *There are two cars in the station car park,* etc.

Extension (30 minutes)

- In pairs, students find a picture in a magazine and write true or false sentences about the picture. Then pairs exchange pictures with another pair and repeat the procedure.

I	don't	you	does	what	is	your	name?	have
have	They	not	we	aren't	from	Japan	are	you
doesn't	stayed	watch	how	can	see	would	you	today?
any	in	TV?	do	can	run?	you	want	coffee?
money	a	leave	you	they	I	like	my	job
does	hotel	why	spell	sing?	like	a	your	is
you	is	what	your	where	swimming	pizza?	why	buy?
lives	you	are	name	do	and	sell	you	eat
in	like	you	please?	live	painting	did	are	There
house?	very	doing	married	you?	pictures	sold	wearing	are
is	happy?	on	there	many	old	new	jeans	two
there	cat	Friday?	How	do	you	are?	and	dogs
why	don't	you	go	to	bed?	friend	a	lunch
can	a	why	your	brother	bought	a	T-shirt	yesterday

14.3

Aim
To match two halves of a text

Language
Review

Skills
Reading and Speaking

Lesson link
Use after Unit 14

Materials
Two copies of the pictures cut up and one copy of the texts cut up per class of twelve students

Answers
Farmer: A and I
Artist: B and K
Student: C and J
Businessman: D and G
Nurse: E and L
Policeman: F and H

Pre-activity (5 minutes)

- Divide students into groups of six and give each group a set of picture cards. Encourage students to try to imagine how each person lives by asking questions, e.g. *What is his/her job? When does he/she get up? When does he/she go to work? When does he/she come home?* etc.

- Have a class feedback session to discuss everybody's ideas.

Procedure (25 minutes)

- Explain to the students that they are each going to read about a typical morning or afternoon of one of the people in the pictures, and that someone else in the class has the other half. Give each student one half of a text. Make sure that everyone has a partner in the class, but that they do not know who their partner is.

- Give students time to read their text and to check any items of vocabulary.

- Now tell the students to imagine that they *are* the person in the text, and they must now find their other half. Students should leave the texts face down on the table, and mingle telling each other about their part of the day. Encourage students to ask questions, e.g. *Where do you work? When do you get up?* Students can go back and look at their text again if they forget anything.

- When a pair of students think they have found their other half, they should go and collect a picture of the person they think they are and both their texts. The students sit down together and check they have found each other correctly. If not they put everything back and start again. If they are correct, they should read both halves of the text together, helping each other to understand everything. Go around listening and helping as necessary.

Extension (15 minutes)

- Put pairs of 'different people' together and tell them to ask each other questions, but this time using the third person form, e.g. *What is his/her job? When does he/she get up?* etc. Again, students try to answer without using the texts, but referring to them if necessary. Go around listening and helping as necessary.

A

In the morning, I usually get up very early, about half past five. I have a cup of tea and some toast. Then I go out and see if the animals are all right. I work for about two hours and then I come in again and have a big breakfast with my wife. She works in the local shop and she leaves the house about nine o'clock. Then I go back to work with the animals. For lunch I have a sandwich, maybe some cheese or eggs or chicken.

I

After lunch I work until about four when my wife comes home from the shop. We have tea together and then we go and work together outside. It is hard work in the winter when it is cold, but it is lovely in the summer. I would never want to work in an office! In the evening we eat at about seven o'clock. Then we read or watch television. We go to bed early because we get up very early. We don't have any children but we want to have some soon.

B

I don't get up early because I work late. I usually get up at about half past nine. I have a cup of coffee and a big breakfast and read the newspaper. Then I work for two or three hours. I look at the pictures I painted the day before and make corrections if there are things I don't like. I don't have a big lunch, usually something small, maybe a sandwich or some soup. After lunch I go for a walk. I like walking and it helps me to have new ideas.

K

After my walk I often visit friends. They are painters or designers, too. We help each other with our work but sometimes we just relax and talk. In the evening I cook dinner quite early, about six o'clock. I like cooking and I especially like Chinese food. Sometimes I cook for my friends. After dinner I work. This is when I do my best work, and I usually work late. Sometimes I work until two o'clock in the morning and I usually get up late!

C

I get up about half past eight. I don't like getting up in the mornings! I would like to stay in bed until ten but I can't. I go to the university at half past nine for my first class. I am studying Mathematics. It is very interesting but difficult! For lunch I eat at the university café. The food is not very nice but it is cheap! I don't have a lot of money. I work part-time in a restaurant to help pay for my university and I would like to buy some new tennis shoes!

J

After lunch I usually go to the library. There are a lot of books I can use to help me study. On Mondays and Thursdays I play tennis. I like tennis very much. After the game I go with my friends to a café or restaurant and have something to eat. Usually we are very hungry then! In the evenings I do many different things. Sometimes I study, especially before an exam! Sometimes I go out with friend. On Fridays and Saturday I work in a restaurant.

D

I get up early every day about seven o'clock. I have a quick breakfast and I leave the house at half past seven. I like to be at work before eight o'clock. In the morning I read my letters and check my e-mails. At nine o'clock I meet with my business partners and we talk about what we are doing that day. It's a very important time. Then I answer my letters and e-mails and have coffee at about eleven o'clock. After coffee I work in the office until lunch time.

G

I usually have lunch in a small restaurant near my office. I go there very often so they know me and always give me a good meal! After lunch I usually leave the office and visit our factory, where we make parts for computers. I talk to the workers and see that everything is OK. Then I come back to the office and work until six o'clock. Sometimes if we have a problem at the factory, I work until seven or eight. In the evening I relax with my family and play with my children.

E

Sometimes I work at night so I start work at eleven o'clock in the evening. I work in a big hospital and I am always busy at work. I finish at seven o'clock in the morning and the first thing I do when I come home is have a big breakfast … or is it dinner? I am very hungry after work because I don't have time to eat very much. Usually I have a sandwich or some fruit.

L

After my breakfast I usually go out and do my shopping. Sometimes I meet friends for coffee or sometimes I go swimming. I come home about twelve o'clock and then I usually read or watch TV. I go to bed about one o'clock but sometimes it is not easy to sleep when the sun is shining! I get up at about eight o'clock and have dinner … or is it breakfast? Then I do my housework and I leave home about ten o'clock. It is funny to go to work when other people are going to bed but I like my job!

F

Good morning! That's what people say to me when I am walking to work. I live in a small village and people know me here. Every morning I usually meet the same people. I get to the Police station about eight o'clock and start on my office work. I work from eight until twelve in the station but I have a coffee break at about half past ten. Then I meet the other officers and we talk about the bad – and good – things in our village.

H

After lunch I go out in to the village. I walk around and now people say 'Good afternoon!' to me! I often help people when they have a problem. I often help tourists when they are lost because I know my village very well. It is a lovely village and people like to come here, especially in summer. At four o'clock I go back to the station and I write down everything that I did or saw that afternoon. At five o'clock I go home and enjoy the evening with my wife and three children!